ECLIPSED HUES

A COLLECTION OF LIFE'S EVOLVING TAPESTRY

ANAHA

Made with ❤ on the Notion Press Platform
www.notionpress.com

To my grandparents, Kamala Hampana and Hampana, with love.

Contents

Contents

Preface

This book contains a collection of poems which are a reflection of the defining years of my life, written between my early teens and early twenties. These were years filled with growth, challenges, and discovery, and they are captured here in poems that explore sadness, love, hardship, and the beauty of life's quieter moments

Many of the poems in this book were born out of difficult times, exploring feelings of grief, heartache, and personal struggle. At other times, the poems reflect on love, nature, and the fleeting joys that life offers. There are gaps in this journey—almost 5 years when I stepped away from writing—but eventually, I returned to it, and this collection is the result of that path back.

Each poem represents a piece of my story, and together they reflect the ups and downs of life, growth through adversity, and the search for meaning. I hope that through these poems, you find something that resonates with your own experiences and emotions.

Acknowledgements

I am deeply grateful to my mum, whose support and love have been the foundation of my writing journey. From the very beginning, when you would take me to the park as a six-year-old and encouraged me to write poems and stories, you planted the seeds of my passion for writing. Your encouragement and your continuous support throughout this entire publishing journey have been invaluable. Thank you for helping me cultivate my love for writing from such a young age.

I am also profoundly grateful to my best friend Arvind, who has been my poetry companion and writing partner since I was twelve. Your invaluable feedback, meticulous grammar checks, and shared enthusiasm for poetry (even when I stopped writing for years) have greatly enriched my work. Your companionship has been a source of joy and inspiration throughout this journey. Your constant support has made this journey both enjoyable and enriching. Thank you for being by my side and helping me refine and perfect my poems.

This book is also a tribute to my grandparents, whose legacy as esteemed writers in Kannada and English has profoundly influenced me. I dedicate this work to my beloved grandmother, who recently passed away. She was also the very first person to have made me immortal through her poems. My grandparent's remarkable contributions to literature continue to inspire me. To my entire family of writers and architect, your creative spirit and support have been a beacon of inspiration throughout my life.

A special thanks to Divyang and all the incredible people I've worked with. Your constant encouragement, help, and the time off you gave me to work on this book have been key to making this possible. I would also like to thank all my close friends who were my rock and support system throughout this entire journey. Thank you all for believing in me.

Last but not the least, I want to extend my deepest thanks to my friends and Instagram followers who took the time to engage with me during live sessions. Your input helped me make crucial decisions and improve this book.

Thank you all for helping me make my dream a reality.

1. BLACK STUDDED HAT

As I walked down the road,

full of people I know,

my eyes hidden behind my black studded hat,

trying to blink away the tears

that are trying to take control.

A drop slowly slides down my cheek,

as I quickly wipe it away.

Fake smile on these lips of mine,

that just wants to shout

and let out the painful things buried deep within,

which wound the scars of mine,

in the same spot over and over again.

My friends don't notice,

as they think I am in a hurry.

I don't want to see the people I love,

or those who love me in return.

Because I know if I do,

there is nothing I can do

to stop my eyes from taking control

and showing how hurt I truly am.

2. WHISPERS OF THE SUMMER BREEZE

Darling, listen to the chirping birds,
flapping from tree to tree.
Their tiny beaks and soft feathers all in our direction,
looking at us with marble-like eyes
that gleam in the light,
which scatters itself through the leaves.
Eyes that sparkle like black diamonds in the light.
I am lost for a second looking at those eyes
that are looking back at me.
As the warm summer breeze slowly weaves through my hair,
it chirps at me as though telling me a long-lost tale.

3. LAND OF SORROW

Lost in my land of sorrow so deep,
Unable to breathe or weep,
Afraid to get lost in a way I can't be found.
I hold on till I can't get around.
I look around hoping to see a ray of light,
To help me find a way out of this immortal night.
A way out of this heart-blinding darkness,
Which has me bound to it so tight,
It's getting hard to fight.
Fight against this life that I'm leading,
For people like to see me bleeding.
As I bleed out the tears from my eyes,
I'm left there weeping.
This overrated smile of mine,
Merely just existing.
Tired of living behind this mask of mine,
And all I do is keep hoping,
Hoping to see a ray of light,
To help me escape this land I find myself lost in.

4. HAUNTED MEMORIES

How can you truly move on when you see the ghosts of your

past,

Everywhere you go?

Tiny pieces of them popping up uninvited in your head,

Like they own the place.

The ghosts of them so real,

It's like they stepped out of your mind,

And are standing right in front of you.

Sitting right in front of you,

Smiling in that restaurant we used to frequent so often,

It became our adda.

Laughing at the stupidest jokes,

That were too lame to be funny.

Crying on that rainy day in August,

As I wiped your tears.

How do you erase the ghosts that have invaded your mind,

Like it's theirs to own?

5. A FEELING LEFT UNDEFINED

One thing I have realized is:

I'm not scared of pain,

I embrace it.

I'm not scared of sadness,

I embrace it.

I'm not scared of happiness,

I embrace it.

I'm not scared of anger,

I embrace it.

But it's the feeling of disgust that I can't embrace.

It's the one feeling that I run away from,

Though it follows close behind,

Lingering like an unspoken shadow,

A darkness I leave undefined.

6. EXIT WOUNDS

So, tell me,

How are your exit wounds?

The wounds that were left on you,

When each person walked out of your life.

Are they as massive as a meteor crater,

Or are they burn marks that you place a cold pack on every

day?

Tell me,

Are you taking care of the wounds and trying to heal them,

Or are you picking at them every time they show any sign of

healing?

Tell me,

Are the questions better left unanswered,

Or do you have a perfectly made-up lie

To cover up for questions you can't answer?

7. FLOODING MEMORIES

I close my eyes and travel back through time.

Only the joyful memories come in front of my eyes.

The last evening of ours,

When we sat on the terrace and stared into infinity.

That was something I will always crave for.

Your eyes sparkled that night,

As though they had something to say-

Something words could never express.

But as I stared back at them, I could read them word by word,

Letter by letter.

Your smile hid a sorrow that you knew was coming true.

But don't take me for a fool,

'Cause I could read it like an open book,

I could read you like an open book.

Those emotions that flooded through your eyes,

Now flooded mine.

As I sail back to reality-

I gasp for air,

As though I almost drowned

In those emotions that flooded the air.

8. PAIN STRUCK EYES

You were happy but sorrow seemed to linger,

Making every minute last,

Trying to capture every minute detail of the night.

Afraid to miss out on something,

Afraid to miss out on anything.

Making every second count,

You were worried,

You were scared—

Not about yourself but about somebody else.

Hope in your eyes,

Prayers in your mind.

Wishing for the best,

Not for yourself but for somebody else.

In your eyes, behind fear,

I could see crystal clear,

Your love for your dear.

But when you laid your eyes on mine,

The fear crept into pain,

And the love for your dear

Started screaming my name.

9. THE BOUGAINVILLEA

Oh, the bougainvillea! It has wrapped itself around the tree

like a beautiful pink gem-studded necklace

around the most beautiful neck you would have ever seen.

As I lay here on my back

under the low-lying leaves of the tree,

As delicate golden rays enrich my soul,

To open my eyes and absorb

the priceless beauty all around me.

The vibrant birds chirping,

the trees dancing,

the warm breeze blowing.

What a place to be lying about.

Oh, what a place to be lying about.

Then I see him,

I see him looking at me.

Those chocolate-brown eyes that resemble the tree's bark

glistened in their own shine.

He walks to me slowly

as I ask myself

if God could have created anyone more mesmerizing than him.

He stole my heart at the first glance.

As I drag my eyes away from him,

I hear him say hi.

We talk, and I get lost in the puzzling feelings of love.

Day in, day out, we met at that same serene place.

The feeling that this is forever

building up within me.

Until one day, when I woke up on the wrong side of the bed,

he vanished into thin air,

making me feel like all that we ever had

was just an enchanting dream.

Days, months, and years have passed.

The feeling that the bougainvillea

is the only thing that can bring him back to me.

The feeling of love that always grows toward him

remained evergreen.

10. UNANSWERABLE QUESTIONS

As I wrestled at night, tossing and turning in bed,

waiting for sleep to embrace me,

I found myself thinking of you,

asking you questions I know I will never get the answers to,

at least not in this life.

So tell me,

how are you?

Have you had the chance to eat the sweets you loved so dearly,

not so long ago?

Do you miss the ones you had to leave behind,

the ones who had your heart,

and the one who was the sparkle in your eye?

Is it dark where you are right now,

or is it filled with light and beautiful days?

Are you lonely in that unfamiliar place,

or are you surrounded by your loved ones who passed on

before you?

Most of all, I wonder,

what were the memories that played through your head in the

last seven minutes before your brain finally gave up?

Ironic, isn't it?

How all of a sudden we have so many things to talk about,

but you're not here to talk to.

11. WINDOW OF MEMORIES

The teacher is teaching something,

something I can't help but not care about.

I look at her face and the board;

well, for me, they both have the same blank faces.

I yawn and look outside the window.

The tree is swaying about, and a cool breeze is blowing.

The new tender leaves have a greenish-yellow color.

The resting raindrops on the leaves

look like diamonds sparkling and reflecting the sunlight.

As a bird sits on the branch,

the droplets shower down.

The bird sits there singing,

as though showing off that it can sing while I can't.

As the bird slowly flaps away,

I see them—

a boy and a girl sitting together,

laughing hand in hand,

resting on each other.

That sparkle in their eyes when they look at each other.

How happy they are, lost in their own world.

Then I think of you;

all our memories flash in my head.

I take one last glance at them
before the teacher tells me to concentrate.
I apologize and try to do as instructed,
but I fail to do so,
as I catch myself looking outside the window
at the happy couple yet again,
your laughter ringing in my head.
The bell rings,
rings to set me free,
free from these memories I am held captive in.

12. TINTED HEARTS

Well, I warned everyone of your name,
And who was to say I'd be the one
who'd fall for this game—
This game of twos spiralling into ones.
Meticulous I stayed,
But the cards you played
Were the ones I craved.
That perfectly toasted skin,
And that perfectly masculine voice.
Who could have ever saved me
From walking into my own demise?
Our perfectly cornered spots
And our perfectly innocent talks,
That we knew were dancing with skillful sinfulness.
It's the roles we play,
That we hope will help us stay
Within the bounds we've bound
Across our untamed hearts.
Tinted we stay,
But between the two of us,
Untinted we remain,
Trying to steal moments of togetherness
Within moments of loneliness.

We are two tinted hearts

Forced to be tinted dark,

Or maybe,

Who is to say if you are truly

What you seem to portray?

13. TEAR-WRAPPED FIRE

So many unused pages,
So many untold stories,
Hidden like always.
These secrets I shall forever withhold,
I shall never unfold.
So many unexpressed feelings
And so many unsaid words,
Left to echo in the darkness,
Hurting like always.
Fire and tears in the eye—
If I look you in the eye,
It's either my want to kill you
Or keep you forever by my side.

14. MULTI-STORIED MASTERPIECE

Building up hope like a multi-storied building,
brick by brick,
word by word,
imagination making it reach the sky.
Waiting for the masterpiece being constructed
to be completed.
Day in and day out,
picturing how things will be.
And when the last brick fits,
your hopes are crushed,
like a snail under the wheels of a car.
Then the building collapses,
and you're standing within,
within the multi-storied edifice
you foolishly built for yourself.
Having nowhere to run, nowhere to go,
it collapses on you,
and you're left to feel the sharp pains all over.
You're left there to bleed to death
without a ray of light coming to your help.
You, beneath this multi-storied masterpiece
you foolishly built for yourself.

15. THE TSUNAMI WITHIN

As I stand here among the ripples of the ocean inside me,

the ripples I have created for myself,

tears streaming down my face,

I cry.

Anger, pain, disappointment, and disgust

are all I seem to feel nowadays—

anger, pain, disappointment, and disgust at myself.

They say a flap of a butterfly's wing at the right time

can cause a tsunami.

Well, this decision of mine was the one flap

that was perfectly timed.

But now I'm drowning,

sinking to the bottom of the sea

due to the tsunami that has flooded

over my self-love and self-respect.

I find it hard to love myself anymore,

because of the way I'm acting now.

For I have become a disappointment to myself.

16. BURNING IN THE GLOW

We can never grow back to how we were before,

because you have shown me

more than a million times

that I'm just going to hurt myself every time I go back to you.

I'm a fool to have never learned.

No matter how many times you hurt me,

the words you speak,

the things you say,

make me want to go back to you.

But now your magical words are slowly losing their spell on me,

because I have now come to see

that you and I are nothing but a moth drawn to a flame,

where you're the glowing, enchanting flame,

and I'm the moth fascinated by it.

The moth, hurting itself every time it touches the flame,

is just going to burn itself in the end.

17. GIRL IN THE MIRRIOR

There she is, looking at something but yet nothing.

She is staring into oblivion,

as millions of things run through her head.

She blinks,

blinks without her knowledge.

I am looking at her,

wondering what she may be thinking.

Then I realize something,

something so sudden that I am woken,

woken from the deep thoughts I was lost in.

I realize that the girl is me.

18. CAPTIVATED ATTENTION

I can feel you walking,

walking behind me.

As you walk up the steps and sit there,

not once do you glance away from me.

Your eyes, fixed on me, refuse to move away.

Even though I don't look at you,

I can feel your eyes on me.

I don't look at you as I know you're desperate for me to do so.

I sit down and continue reading, and you continue staring.

As I get up to leave,

you call my name in tiny whispers.

I wait for you to call me a few more times,

just to listen to your voice say my name over and over.

Then I look at you with a smile

A smile as soft as the moment itself,

and you say bye.

While I climb down the steps,

I hear your faint whisper of, "See you soon." linger in the air.

Like it's a secret only meant for you.

19. DREAMS

I miss you,

I miss you every time I blink.

You're the dreams I dream of at night.

You're the thoughts I think of day in and day out.

As I open my eyes every morning,

the urge to cuddle back in bed fills up within me,

the urge to cuddle back in bed

just to be able to be with you,

at least in my dreams.

As that is all I have of you,

you in my dreams.

HUE

20. HUE-1

Eating has become a Herculean task, yet again.
I can't seem to keep food inside of me, yet again.
Everything is turning into a blurry dream, yet again.
Those charcoal-painted clouds have taken over, yet again.
Memories slipping away like a fleeting dream, yet again.
Will this gyration ever really stop? I wonder.
How long can I keep surviving this cycle? I ponder.

21. HUE-2

I go through joy,

I go through pain.

But when joy ends, I wish it would return.

But when pain ends, I hope it never returns.

But without pain, we wouldn't know what joy is.

Together they live side by side,

And what divides them is a small line the size of a hair strand.

22. HUE-3

I tend to believe that the most cheerful-looking people are the
saddest,
As they don't want to answer to the world why they aren't,
While they are struggling to just inhale and exhale.
They try to squeeze out as much of happiness as they possibly
can
From the smallest of moments, just to survive.

23. HUE-4

"When you are not showered with love,
You learn to lick it off of knives," they say.
But that's the thing about tongues, isn't it?
Always hidden and tucked safely away,
So that the cuts and scars can stay secret, safe.
Yet every taste of love or pain is a harsh reminder,
Of the cuts that never truly healed.

24. HUE-5

I have experienced many miracles in life,
And you were my favorite.
But that's the funny thing about miracles—
They don't last very long.
So I thank the universe for
Giving me a miracle I so lovingly call by your name,
Wherein we created our own tiny glimpses of magic
That no one can erase.

25. HUE-6

The one unwavering truth is that
We never would have worked,
In this timeliness or any other,
No matter how much I wanted it to.

26. HUE-7

Doesn't it almost always start with a "Hi"
And end with a lie?
My lie was that I didn't care,
Whereas yours was that you did.

27. HUE-8

Don't fill up your heart with those who couldn't love it,
Fill it with those who did.
For they are the ones worthy
Of the love and pain that radiates within you.

28. HUE-9

Was I so insignificant to your vision
That you could not make out my sadness?
Could you not see the tears I was shedding?
My voice, barely making its way out?

29. HUE-10

You could have shot me in the heart

And walked away,

But you shot my knee caps off.

You shot me where it hurts the most

And left me there in excruciating pain.

Whereas all I ever did was try to share the burden of yours.

30. HUE-11

Isn't it ironic how we live in denial
At a person's passing,
But jump right into grief
At the loss of a someone very much alive?

31. HUE-12

I think the feeling of loneliness
is the universe's way
of making you realize
you've been holding onto something
past its expiration date.

32. HUE-13

His murky brown eyes said so much,
But now I realize, they were all just lies—
Lies told to deceive me and my tender heart.

33. HUE-14

And if I can't have love, I hope to have power.

Because, in the end, isn't love just another word for power?

A feeling more powerful than power itself?

34. HUE-15

I spoke of you like you created the world,
While you burnt my whole existence down to mere ashes.